Natalie and the Night Sky

Written by Carolyn Dibb

Illustrated by Kent McAlister

Balboa Press books may be ordered through booksellers or by contacting:

Balboa Press
A Division of Hay House
1663 Liberty Drive
Bloomington, IN 47403
www.balboapress.com
1 (877) 407-4847

ISBN: 978-1-5043-2689-6 (sc)
ISBN: 978-1-5043-2690-2 (e)
Library of Congress Control Number: 2015900963

Print information available on the last page.

Balboa Press rev. date: 04/22/2015

BALBOA

For Anna

Preface

To the Parents

The reasons parents have only one child are as varied as the parents themselves. My hope is that this book boosts your child's feelings of being cherished and connected in this world.

Warmly,
Carolyn Dibb, M.Ed.

Natalie is having the best summer of her life.

Tonight she is camping with her best friend Shayla and both of their families. Natalie knows that she and Shayla will be friends forever after this big adventure.

Natalie looks across the roaring campfire at her friend. Shayla's face is covered from nose to chin in melty chocolate from the yummy smores. Steven, Shayla's older brother, is sitting next to her roasting marshmallows over the fire. Steven leans over and whispers something to Shayla and they both start giggling.

Natalie gets up, moves around the circle, and plops into the seat next to Shayla. Shayla and Steven are giggling uncontrollably.

"What's so funny?" Natalie asks them.

Steven leans over and between gasps of air from laughing says "My Dad….teaching us to fish…..slipped….fell into river……soaking wet…..from about a foot of water."

Natalie looks at the brother and sister with tears running down their faces from laughing so hard. She starts to giggle in spite of herself. Their laughter is so contagious.

After a little while, they settle down again. They all watch the fire glowing in the darkness. Steven goes back to the business of roasting marshmallows over the fire. Shayla gives Natalie a lopsided grin and then shakes her head as her brother loses yet another marshmallow into the fire.

There is something that Natalie really wants to ask Shayla, but she doesn't know how.

"Ah, Shayla," Natalie says quietly leaning in closer to her friend, "I was just wondering, do you like having a brother?"

Shayla looks surprised by Natalie's question. She thinks about it for a moment and says, "It's good and bad. I like it when he helps me with my homework or when we go biking together, but I hate it when he teases me. Oh, he also eats all the cookies in the house! By the time I have one cookie he has had three!" Shayla says annoyed.

Natalie looks over at Steven as he squishes two whole smores together and shoves them into his mouth. She shakes her head and laughs.

Shayla leans over to her friend and whispers, "Natalie, why do you ask? Do you wish you had a brother or a sister?"

Natalie shrugs and says "I'm not sure. Sometimes, I think it might be nice to have a brother or a sister to hang out with. It is usually just me, Mom and Dad."

Shayla gives Natalie a big hug and declares "Well,
I'll hang out with you anytime you like."

Natalie's heart fills with the words from her friend, but still
she wonders; what it would be like to have a brother or sister?
It is starting to get late and Shayla's Mom calls for her to
come back to the tent. She sighs and shrugs her shoulders
then waves goodbye to Natalie. Natalie watches brother and
sister race after each other as they leave the campfire.

Natalie looks up at the dark sky and is filled with amazement at the ocean of stars above her.

"Penny for your thoughts?" asks Natalie's Dad.

Natalie grins and snuggles in close to him
as he sits in the chair beside her.

"Dad, there are so many stars up there. Do you think they are all brother and sister stars?" she wonders.

Her Dad smiles, "I am sure a lot of them are, but I think there also might be a few Mom and Dad stars, some Gran and Grandpa stars, maybe a smattering of Uncle, Aunt and Cousin stars." he teases.

"Oh Dad." Natalie exclaims, giving him a little nudge.

Natalie's Dad looks at her as she watches Shayla and her brother playing a game of cards inside their tent.

"You know Natalie, there is a very special set of three stars in the night sky. It is called the Summer Triangle and if you look just over there, you can see it."

Natalie looks to where her Dad is pointing, but she can't really see a triangle in amongst all the other stars.

"Just a second", her Dad says and he pulls a piece of paper and a pen out of his pocket. He starts to draw stars all over the page.

He shows her the brightest star in the triangle called the Vega. He then maps out the rest of the constellation.

As Natalie's Dad draws on the paper she starts to see the triangle as if he were drawing it right in the sky for her.

"Now, the Summer Triangle is a very special family of stars. There is the Mom star, the Dad star and the beautiful daughter star. You can see they form a very tight little triangle and are very close to each other. But one of the neatest things about the triangle is; do you see how many stars surround it and are in the middle of it?" he asks.

Natalie nods.

"It is kind of like families. There might only be a few members in a particular house, but the world is full of extended family stars, best friend stars and almost-like-a-sister stars."

"So even though a family might look small, when you look around, you will see they are connected in a bigger way with other people; just like the stars in the sky."

Natalie thinks about this quietly for a minute.

"Dad, are you or Mom *ever* sad that it is just the three of us?" Natalie asks.

"Not for one moment," her Dad declares. "You are my Natalie, the brightest, shiniest, most precious star and we feel so lucky that you completed our triangle."

Natalie gives her Dad a hug.

"Now," her Dad says, "How about we head back to the tent for a game of gin rummy with Mom?"

Natalie smiles and nods.

Natalie looks around the busy campground at her friends and family settling down for the night. The tents are glowing like stars, a little bit like her own constellation on the ground. Then Natalie looks up at the sea of stars covering the sky, finds the Summer Triangle sitting just above the horizon and smiles.

The End

About the Author

First and foremost, Carolyn Dibb is an avid reader. Her love
of good stories blossomed as a young girl and continues to
this day. Reading nightly to her own child inspired her to start
writing life skills books for kids. Carolyn has a Master's degree in
counselling psychology from the University of British Columbia.
She currently resides with her family in Western Canada.

www.carolyndibb.com

Acknowledgments

To my lovely husband Warren, your love and support have given me the confidence to see this project through. Thank you also for the many, many rereads I subjected you too.

To my good friend and talented editor Nicole, your comments and insights added so much to this book. Thank you my friend!

To my dear friend Kent, thank you for doing the beautiful illustrations. They truly enrich the book. Who knew that 35 years after our first meeting we would create a book together!

To my parents, Gordon and Sheryl, who are always a constant source of encouragement and support. Thank you for always being there to cheer me on and lend a helping hand in any way you can.

Lastly, to my little one, who always insists we read at least five books at bedtime and secretly hopes she can push it to 10! It is my time with you that inspired me to write a children's book. You have boundless creativity and are such a joy.

CPSIA information can be obtained at www.ICGtesting.com
Printed in the USA
LVOW05s2357070515

437343LV00026BA/327/P